MY FATHER'S EYES WERE BLUE

My Father's Eyes Were Blue

First edition © The Heaventree Press 2009
All work © Antony Owen 2009
All rights reserved
ISBN 978-1-906038-36-6

Cover art: 'Covdusk' © Kris Connolly 2009
Heaventree logo design by Panna Chauhan

Published in the UK by
The Heaventree Press,
Institute for Creative Enterprise,
Puma Way, Coventry Technology Park
CV1 2TT

Printed in the UK by
Cromwell Group, Trowbridge, Wiltshire BA14 0XB

We are grateful for the financial support of ARTS COUNCIL ENGLAND

MY FATHER'S EYES WERE BLUE

Antony Owen

The Heaventree Press

ACKNOWLEDGEMENTS

On the long road to getting these poems into print, I have met many people I wish to thank: my inspirational English teacher Andy Taylor at Coundon Court School ("my captain, my captain!"); my family for their support; my beautiful wife, Joanne; my two brothers, David and Richard, for their reality checks; Jon Morley, for those caffeine-induced writing sessions and for creating the Nightblue Fruit poetry evenings, a catalyst for opportunity where so many of these poems were tested out; Lorraine and Gary Drinkwater, for sponsoring the print run; and Gilbert Gigliotti, David Gallagher, Barry Patterson, Jacqui Rowe, Paul Casey, Martin Green, Colin Dick, Jane Commane and Kirsten Mackintosh for their encouragement.

Always & Forever

Exquisite Wedding Flowers & Hand-made Stationery

From feathers and sparkle, to hand-tied and traditional, we can help you create exactly what you want!

Always & Forever offers you a service all under one roof… from your stationery right through to the confetti on your tables!

Call Lorraine to arrange a free consultation. She can make your wedding day dreams become a reality, at realistic prices!

Email: always_forever@hotmail.co.uk
Tel: 024 7654 1912

for Joanne Owen

CONTENTS

Half Moon on Hannover Street	11
Nests Eagles And Lovers Leave	12
Rats	13
Forgiveness	14
The Second Destruction Of Coventry	16
Spiders and Butterflies	17
Milk and Gas	18
New Nagasaki	19
Prelude to an Infidelity	20
Field over Choeung Ek	21
Ribbon Creek	22
Monsters in Ladybirds	23
Clam	24
Portals	25
Marrakech	26
Divorced Children	27
Thierry and the Moon	28
The Coventry Hangings, 1765	29
Nights at the Skydome	30
Stone	31
Spon End Subway	32
John Grace Street	33
Porcelain	34
Carlos Huarrez	35
My Blue Lover Rages	36
The Bludgeoning Quilt	37
Echoes of Eichmann	38
By Shelves Of My Father's Shed	39
Her Name Was Marjorie Harper	40
The Life That Went On	41
Water	42
The Copper Man	43
White Picket War	44
The Runt	45
Woman of the Rocks	46
Old River Sherbourne	47
223, Browns Lane	48
The Cowardice Of Francis Evans	49

My Father's Eyes Were Blue	51
The Dance Before Dunkirk	52
Keyhole to a Closed Door	53
Aeroplanes and Fledglings	54
The Watch and the Hiding	55
Apricots	56
Letter from Palermo	57
The Spider and the Wife	58
Cigarette Starlet	59
Leaving Crane's Records	60
The Other	61
Harvest Moon	62
The January Dogs	63
Room 17, Ashford Hospital	64
Six Million Stars	65
Flatline	66
Blackbird In Bed	67
Hiroshima, 8:12am	68
Unbroken Horses	69
Childhood Wedding	70
Blood and Battenberg	71
The White Disciple	72
Kefalonia	73
Foxgloves	74
Lost Shadows	75
Monologues	76
Sunrise on the Slag Heap	77
Corner Shop, Quinton Road	78

Half Moon on Hannover Street

for Richard and Kelly

In your womb rainbow
he looked like black grain.
A mouthless doctor spoke
of how to breathe in July
when the flower unfurls.

I stitched his name in silver,
kept him safe in Latin yachts
breathing towards the sky
northward to cumulus shores:
he arrived still as moon.

July saw his rebirth,
a half moon on Hannover Street.
I kissed his mother there
beneath swan-necked lampposts.

In the space between our lips
he fastened a family of three
from two breaths and a name
we could finally say together.

Nests Eagles and Lovers Leave

Twilight drags a darkened hem
like Kefalonian widows
to whitewashed nests
yielding to a phoenix' nest
the Eagles left.

She cries like Messerschmidts
to a wind of beaks
for the way he smiled at her
deep in the Argostoli hills,
bark engraving her back
leaving a nave
where his mouth nested.

Daylight drags its golden swords
slitting guilt from her throat
to bleed in myriads on the floor
she kept cleansing.

There are too many widows
with bodies as open graves,
with gold hems leaving shadows
where lips have met with knaves.

Rats

Throat slit red
in brakelight trance
my twelve-hour changeling
appears in wing-mirror sunrise
heralded by birds in tarmac trees.

Traffic light duel:
Audi versus Saab,
amber green smog.
Third exit grave,
parking among the failures
in Hyundai badges.

Eleven hours crawl.
Rats scurry one on another
gnawing.

Rob is now Robert,
rat is now mouse.
At twenty past nine
by mute tarmac trees
my rat sleeps in its Saab tomb

until it wakes again on my forehead
crawling into my mouth.

Forgiveness

Courage left you today,
your husband for so long.
my wife is now memories;
I am married to mirrors of regret.

Forgive me for my weakness.

The times you walked on your own
asking in laptop grey—
I ignored you for a client
who always spelled my name wrong.

Forgive me for my ignorance.

The day of the envelope
when you were different
by being too much the same to me,
for I was indifferent to you.

Forgive me for my blindness.

The day you lit candles at noon,
stood naked next to them
and asked me if you were beautiful
saying my full name.

Forgive me for shaking.

The day you told me was a Sunday:
later you said you had waited for a frost
just like the first walk we ever took
when there was bonfire and love in my eyes.

Forgive me for hating you.

The day you lost your hair
refusing to wear a headscarf
choosing to wear the elements—
the wind, the rain and when we kissed, a smile.

Forgive me for loving you too much.

The days I stayed with you to the end,
noticed everything I hadn't done
except for the only thing you wanted:
to dance with you to Jared,
you went in my arms from the flute's first breath...

I'll never forgive you for that.

The Second Destruction of Coventry

At City Arcade's helm
an imprisoned Gypsy wind
swoops past a displayed massacre
of pork bellies and shop owners,
bringing a stench of trade death.
Its odour: shoe leather,
Costa Rican coffee beans
and deadline;
ripping the ivory tusks
from a sky blue elephant
slaughtered for a white one.

The truth is cold
as a lap dancer's thigh.
The commercial harlot
in her blue and yellow robe
looks to her cowering pimps
with their open laptops
and Jerde logo pens
who bow to Starbucks
and close the shutters
of Barrington's café
and Gemma's wool shop.

Soon at City Arcade
the air will be golden
in a slab cold wind.
Where canaries used to sing
a JCB will richter
Coventry slain by logos
and commercial Luftwaffe
shall bomb us with slogans—
who will pick up the cross?

Spiders and Butterflies

Tied in silk
it weaved a trap,
watched your demise,
drained our insides
and watched us fall
in the glint of raindrops.

Love is a predator—
it enters as butterflies
and leaves as a spider
on a ground of still wings,
a cud of spewed hearts.

From the air of its fluttering
at least we breathed—
saw its short lived beauty soar
then spin like silk and sycamore.

Milk and gas

The Fulbright scholar
rubbed herself like Vim
around twelve day footprints
facing towards "the other".

Hair crowded her temples
once worshipped by quill.
Two spines,
one falling apart,
one almost complete.

She scrubbed away his footprints,
finding her father's face.
Wolves stood up to the moon,
she stood up to the stove
embracing gas like a Nazi.

Milk was poured in a half empty glass
for half empty children.

New Nagasaki

Nagasaki smog gown
brakelight snake light
wing-mirror sundown

Nagasaki moon nape
plane scars crane stars
neon logo sky-scrape

Nagasaki sunrise
mandarin peels cantering heels
rush-hour dragonflies

Fat Man tumbling
flash face sash lace
shadow strumming

Prelude to an Infidelity

At the end of the street
where the cold wind is stolen
by the kebab shop
my jacket turned green
and Tchaikovsky brought my wife
vibrating from my pocket
in a chariot of light.

The old doorman coughed
hocking phlegm into a silk handkerchief.
Rain filled his pockmarks,
his smile insincere
as a Chelsea man's handshake—
vicelike, tepid.

Check-in desk pseudonym,
walnut-reflected devil
and crumbling from an East London voice:
Sign 'ere and 'ere, love.

Doused by her bleached meat
a painted noose strangled me.
When I kissed her chest
Jesus danced on a silver noose
falling into my mouth
with a taste of bitter metal.

Field over Choeung Ek

In Novotel blue
a temple French-smokes;
this Marlboro suckling
fans thin Buddhas
to good time Englishmen
in Tuc Tuc plumes.

Last night
in joss stick vapours
prayer smoke transported her
to acres of lemongrass,
bowing to her
as she ran in zigzags
the way she was taught
in the skull years.

Fields are kerbs now
bringing bartering shadows
of vulgar dialects,
back alley exaltations:
his thigh hairs lemongrass
from her Khmer Rouged hands.

Two thousand prayers away
a field of lemongrass
will be etched with zigzags,
and her thighs will tremble
like pollen over Choeung Ek.

Ribbon Creek

I was five and ancient,
my throat pieced by
your face of a thousand knives
and rubies on my cheeks.

My red dressing gown
in strip-lit dark:
the cord was a snake
until Dad coughed
changing it back to a cord.

He never smiled much
yet when he did
my sadness was like corn
bowing to his hand
for his ivory scythe
made me stomp in sandals again
to a creek of sorrow-stones
where he talked about Mum leaving
and of the rivers that lead
to vast oceans.

Monsters in Ladybirds

When I was a child
scabs were fun wounds,
parents were pain wounds;
when I was a child
coughs brought cloves
and cloves brought guardians
with dead dreamers' books
of wolves and damsels
tucked in warm linen.

When I was a child
life was as still as
ladybirds on lifelines
yet when they opened their wings
a monster stole their spots
and I wiped my fear on the mud
I now know as adulthood.

When I was a child
the moon wasn't blind to me;
I saw robins at Christmas,
wore hugs like parkers
the rain like Kate Moss
and the world was a snowglobe
covered in my fingerprints.

Clam

A lacerating tide
brings a boy face-down,
mourned by gulls' echoes:

a boy from a slag heap heart
fastening against a warm breast of the shingle,
blue embers aglow from coal
and broken-veined waters
dirtying his rock pool eyes.

Portals

Portals to you are
a sleeve of eyes
from when I last held you:
our twelfth goodbye.

Portals to you are
Stratford on Avon,
a downloaded mortuary
of black-and-white hedgerows.

Portals to you are
the ruby grave of whispers,
vow's lost jewel
which died on your lips.

Marrakech

I take my seven days,
paint each of them tazetta.
You take Monday
painting a watercolour
of blue and weeping.
Your Daddy's shell, leaving harbour
like trawlers, by moonlight.
Fish gill, net death:
pulsing silver mountains
on a starboard of scales
by Daddy's stench bucket.

Touch me with ten tombstones,
wake the dead in me,
love me like a dog:
we need each other.

Yasmine candles
took us back to Marrakech,
and through their burning
you remembered how we were,
and that one night in eight years
you painted our son yellow
and devils and daddies slept
until death's watercolour brought
your cod eye glance
facing east, unanchored.

Divorced Children

You learnt from your duvet
that your Mum had left,
hunting detergent to smell
so she could comfort you,
the seventies woodchip lamp
glowing through the gap in the door she left.

You learnt from the kitchen
that your Dad would stay
to pick up the pieces that were you
and Simon who'd wet himself for soft hands
while you and the compensatory dolls waited
for the gap in the door to creak again.

You learnt how to raise yourself,
then later on there were lovers
who'd love themselves through you.
Affection was an exorcism
ending in a slammed door
and a gap in your life.

You learnt from your Dad
that your Mum was a whore,
that lies were shouts,
truths were whispers
and children forced to be adults
dragged across the common
in shoes too small for them
and lives too big for them.

I learnt from you
that life is those shoes you wore;
that I can never fill them
the way you do my heart.

Thierry and the Moon

I remember my friend Thierry
waiting on an orange ball
for his name to be called.
Every day he waited to be picked
and when he scored
Tutsi and Hutu clashed only in smiles
unless it was a draw.

I remember my friend Thierry,
waiting in his father's suit
for his father's bones.
That night his village danced
and Thierry plucked the moon,
placed her in my Tutsi palms—
I dried his eyes with the moon.

I remember Thierry
waiting for the United Nations
to leave the church I was blessed in.
Every day he waited by the fence
and when he killed
Hutu and Tutsi clashed only in tears.
Everybody lost.

I remember Thierry
waiting for my Mama,
my brother
and my baby Jamila.
I will not forget my Rwanda
for I buried her with my head
in hands by godless graves.

The Coventry Hangings, 1765

Within three eyelets of rope were
pippin blossom and horsehair
and a moaning cart
where six damned eyes
of Coventry blue
would weave themselves white.

From the thousand crowd
a baritone nobleman
greeted them by name,
damned them by moniker,
then lips and lifelines pressed together
before the glockenspiel ascent to death.

Within three eyelets were
"Baker", "Drury" and "Leslie".
A yarn of heads tried to pray—
God replied in gibbet, and
the slow motion ladder
brought August to three buds
of Cofa's tree.

Nights at the Skydome

Black cab cavalcades arrive:
dark vassals in dark vessels
dress cobblestones in H&M shadows,
alcoholic sonnets sounding
"I 'ate paki taxi drivers."

One they call Trish has a scab.
Chinese font emblazons her back:
goddess of ultraviolet,
image in orange
blowing off a bottle of Bud.

Mandy's out for a shag,
scenting chavs' aroma,
the words that melt her ice exterior
"You've got wicked tits, darlin'."
"Not so bad yourself mate."

Three a.m. kerb vultures
peck at dead gazelles,
kebab meat devoured in a Spon Street alley.
Gary gets a blowjob
next to where his mate pissed.

Stone

I remember watching my wife,
breasts against a damson sky,
how they hung like
half-shy daffodils,
hungering for a soft vase—

how consonants travelled
to the wind-chimes,
numb as a fastened breast.

A child cannot be born from stone
when stone is born from a child.

Spon End Subway

A shadow of Thatcherism
grouts post-war subway:
unfragrant ghost of industry
enmeshed in political lathes.
Alsatian-warm,
tenement-grey,
trading Lennon for put-downs
from pinstriped shadows.

In moth-dead flicker
Elizabeth shines
pillowed upon a suede quarry of indignity:
the purifier of conscience,
next to a beaker marked 'McD'
and a clown high on lows
with a name no-one knows.

He hurls a chorus to a neon nymph,
a high heel lyric for twelve bar blues…
four pounds eight pence later
moon turns to foil,
hope to latex
wrapped around an arm
that once made the Daimler.

John Grace Street

Wind left a scent of wine,
elm brushed onto flecked walls
a lovemaking name I wrote
after your argument face.

A chorus of empty coathangers
dresses me in naked truths;
charity clothes steam-ironed
summon lavender ghosts.

Rest upon my shoulder, chuck,
I'll walk you home to John Grace Street,
lie with you until you leave
with my hand in a ring of your hair.

Porcelain

You left our bed a cot—
just me in a throat-heavy quilt
that I would throw off
in favour of your thighs.

We once curled like wicks,
glowing together until you flickered;
your shadow burned on the woodchip,
meshed against the oak outside.

You held me when no arms would—
paper flesh veined with blue,
bones fine as porcelain,
a fraught fragility streaked with salt.
For a time we sipped champagne from teacups
at breakfast every morning,
adding the pearl freshness of fizz
to the steady warmth around our hearts.

I hear you cry from the North through the sill,
a wailing font writes your loss.
I breathe on the window to mock myself,
watching my mouth sew the colour of your flesh,
then I hold myself as you held me
and the man you loved cracks like porcelain
to a changeling who hates you for leaving
and talks to the air about his loss.

I whisper on the wind the tale of my love,
place hands on the window to reach towards you,
see your breath scroll behind the pane
as the world smashes and I am ice.

Carlos Huarrez

In a street named after a nuke
fifty limp stars hang upside down
forty-five yards from the wire fence
where Carlos Huarrez plucked F14s.

Carlos became a marine
looking west from the East
whenever shots hit sand puffing
blue screams from death-shells.

His taker was Kazem from Lahore—
an earthquake made him a soldier.
Once he made boats, and children,
and both he and Carlos held shells
to their children's ears.

Nesting inside a woman Carlos called "Te Amo"
is the boy she'll name after him.
Clasping at the fence
she makes pictures
from wired diamond clouds
waiting for wind to move the flag.

My Blue Lover Rages

On goosebump dunes
brunette waves fell sideward.
Moon weaved a salt frock
of fish-silver.
She swayed in sea-grass
wishing upon a zodiac
of the offshore oil-rig.

We lay numeral
melting from a Dalí clock,
my big hands on your little hands,
our twelfth-hour thighs
announcing a chime of lips.

Storm:
my lover's Atlantic mouth
spumed with driftwood
wrapped in stinking veins.
Cold steamed a ghost ship.
My compass set at north
slipped through my fingers,
facing south to where she frothed
whispering the New World's name.

The Bludgeoning Quilt

I painted my nails for you,
held you like rosary,
tearing your bread of spine apart
wrestling, our sheets stained with Merlot.

I painted my love for you
in lip, lobe and lashes,
my body your abstract expression,
a Pollock of scratches.

Sunrise on yestersheets.
Your foetal nylon mould
wears my mouth banshee,
dancing in a sill wind
by our bludgeoning quilt.

Echoes of Eichmann

I heard he cried
like a baby he shot
that wept for a Gypsy breast
hungering to feed him.

Eichmann left many echoes,
one from a bedroom in Vienna.
Jewflesh softly stamped his chest
making love—
his hands stroking like signatures
on transportation papers.

Eichmann left other echoes,
stamp after stamp pressed by numbers
making hate—
29881 travelled to Sobibor,
left as dry grey rain.

Before the Judas rope
Eichmann's last supper was red wine,
his last echo his neck,
his eyes two silver coins—
cost of the Fatherland
spent by Jewish fists hurling ash
on Mediterranean skin,
a sea that never rests.

By Shelves Of My Father's Shed

Through a half-creosoted door
I left their world ajar.
No one saw the anvil swallow me
as I painted swastikas on tailfins.

I was born like wood-shavings
and Jesus was sick of that smell.
My Dad was born from dust,
so I swept remnants of balsa
into the light that ended
on his crooked shelves.

I heard the otherworld
speak kindly yet ill of him,
inaccurate and lazy words
in mouths filled with sandwiches
quartered for good impression.

In moth-dead flicker
I whispered goodbye,
launched the last Henkel
into his garden of stricken bouquets.
I was five again
me again,
and Jesus was the chisel
of my eyes,
his eyes.

Her Name Was Marjorie Harper

I died a blur in half-moon glasses,
her eyes reflecting the blitz.
I never told the nurse till nine,
holding her in television blue
in remembrance, like Stoke bricks.

A nurse turned her bed:
fresh linen for fresh dead
and the marigold sky
was plucked from a china vase,
jettisoned headfirst into polythene.

Salaried pats from a light hand,
carbon dioxide apologies.
The night nurse offered a mint,
the chaplain offered the Lord
but I took none, just the vase
and a velour dressing gown
with her scent of April.

The Life That Went On

Ten necromancers bewitch her:
he is different to me.
In silver walls I smile
and we hold each other
immortal as nothing,
yet you were everything
when I was mortal.

It took you thirty-five months
yet I faded by the thirteenth.
Memories live in a loft,
lying next to your Mother
and a rush-buy ornament
that you bought me from Tunisia.

His name is Darren Davison.
He drives a BMW,
has a flourishing business
and charmed you into bed
the first night you met him.

You carry his child.
It will be a girl.
You will call her Bethany
and I will watch over you
until she is born,
and then I will leave
returning only as the tears
you cry once a year
on the date we were born.

Water

Born with her water on his face,
freed from umbilical shackles
he was named Madoowbe:
I wanted to share that with you.

His father was a green man.
He left black women red,
life and death in wombs
and kinder death to men from blade.

Madoowbe and his mother walked for water,
taking turns to walk in their shadows
until the shimmering turned blue
and sand was hammered by hooves.

When Madoowbe's mother got sick
she went to the white man, who took her blood:
days later dying with water on her face.
Her name was Jamila,
I wanted to share that with you.

Madoowbe walked for water.
Gazelles had wiped away his mother's footprints.
He took his blind grandmother's hand
spilling water in her mouth:
he wanted to share it with her.

The Copper Man

Somewhere on Mayfair pavements,
amongst the flocking drones,
a jelly-necked vagrant
lay dead on sodden cardboard,
dressed in Versace shadows
and copper they flicked.

His Labrador licked him,
changing from gold to blue,
barking and biting at neon reapers
who took away his master,
muzzling his grief.

Embedded in the vagrant's palm
was a medal from King George.
The pauper box is planed.
Let's just bury him,
shrapnel for our conscience,
and I'm late for my meeting.

White Picket War

Paradise drums
topsy-turvy stars
pavement portals
slave-black sky
from whipped white eye

Bush fire
waterfall
Starbucks deathaccino
smoke-'em-out heroes
la la la la la la Rambo!

War of the necromancers
dial 9/11 for Jesus
767 for Allah
Macarena   Macedonia
Bush dance
war dance

Custer heart and Wounded Knee
washed in crude oil Galilee
home Vietnam-style
Walmart zombie
shaking tins to Mexicans
impaled
on a white picket fence:
Pleasantville

The Runt

I was eight when I discovered
death was jellied and sable;
the bitch licked the still runt
nudging it back to her womb.

Through a lattice of fingers my mother sobbed,
half-watching a bowl-headed woman
come with ether and gloves
uttering "It's only a runt, dear."

She tried to take the runt
but the collie growled and snapped;
its litter suckled her curd,
eight kicking hinds moved the stillborn
towards gloves and grinning molars.

To the collie I walked.
Furring my chaliced palm,
she licked me leaving frothen eyes on my cheek.
My mother took me outside,
told me to wait in the car.

I saw the bowl-headed woman
in a blue montage of sulphur
lighting a furnace,
unrolling the runt,
dousing it in paraffin
then folding the blanket she kept.

We left with four collies that day
as the woman warmed her hands
and the runt was carried north
by a growling wind of ash.

Woman of the Rocks

Friday's death
birthed cider and sodomy
and his indigo brushes
blotted a masterpiece
of tomorrow's regret.

Zombie in the dresser mirror,
grimacing kindling her.
Mascara and concealer
painted over lies,
beautifully covered
in time for tea at Gran's.

Mum poured milk on my cereal,
resembling her cameo.
Dad slept sucking his thumb,
fists furred red
by a gold wedding band
that Grandad had worn happily
for forty-nine years.

Old River Sherbourne

Limbs of Sherbourne crawl
struggling over stones
as tombed with tyres and trolleys
westward she wends
to oil-slaughter from the M6 bowel.

She turns to foam.
A stench of her rises
through fragrant crow-foot
dancing on her grave.

With Canute's defiance she struggles on
past Sandy Lane to weave with Spon
until summer, when she is gone.

223, Browns Lane

I was a child of conifers
            twenty feet tall.

Nothing grows in the greenhouse now—
            raspberries furred to grey
                        wasp-hollowed coxes
blossom   and shards of glass.

Half-buried in compost
gloves rigor-mortis,
point at paraffin lamps
and unrolled woodbines.

            I will leave quietly soon
                        the same way I entered.

The Cowardice of Francis Evans

I watched the frost cry for sunrise,
jewelling the swords of soil.
Dawn gave birth to death
and a corvid choir rejoiced
on the steel giants.

Dawn dances in its white gown
on empty graves dressed in nettles,
the wind has come to moan
the sun has risen to fall
and like the crown of winter's queen
all that lives is all that's green.

My great uncle sleeps here,
shot for cowardice in 1917.
He held his friend's cranium
then held his friend,
took his wedding ring for safekeeping
and hitched a ride to Esbjerg.

He left Esbjerg a soldier of the King,
arrived in Harwich a traitor,
but he lived to complete his vow
and arrived at Ethel's a man.

"William told me to tell you goodbye,"
giving her a pressed thistle.

Ethel remarried and had twelve grandchildren,
my Uncle was captured on his twentieth year,
tied to a plinth with a blindfold
singing "Abide with me"
before he was shot by six children.

Every epitaph tells a story
and my Uncle loved the dawn.
His name was Francis Evans
the fiancé of Margaret,

the father of her miscarriage
and coward revoked 80 years later
by a fat mayor in Warwick.

My Father's Eyes Were Blue

Anvil-eyed, my father glanced at me.
"Dress me well for Karen," he said.
He drew breaths like a Davy lamp
as I brushed his hair with steady hands.

My father was Sicilian.
The miners called him Brando,
my mother called him darling,
and he left for work golden,
returning a shadow
who stained my lips black.

He'd sit by my bed
stroking my hair
coaling my forehead.
I knew he kissed me every night
for I awoke in tattoos
from where he held me,
reading me Whitman while I slept.

He had no last words for me,
just a smile and a squeeze of my hand
and he was twenty-three again,
in a Daimler with Karen
driving to Loch Lomond
with forty-two shillings,
two smiles, two rings
and her father's wrath.

The Dance Before Dunkirk

Tumours mark his back
like the road Dorniers strafed,
the road to Dunkirk.
The unburied
facing away from the sky
belly-down friends.

Six months before
he danced in a talcum cloud
where borrowed nylons
wove foxtrots to his knees,
her lips daubing him
like Dunkirk trees
guiding him home.

Sixteen miles from Dunkirk
in a fog of German tongues
he hid amongst pines
listening to a French song strafing
from a German armoured car.

Tumors mark his back—
he danced to the curtains
with a black-and-white photo—
his lips daubed the glass—
then he slept belly-down
and she guided him home
to a room smelling of pines.

Keyhole to a Closed Door

Sick from her ointment
my flesh amphetamine-dissolved,
pale as a clockface
killing time with closed hands.

Orange mouthed.
Breathing veiled daemons
from the wintered host
coiled frozen from my love's warmth,
mutilating half of her
and all of me.

My gift lies unwrapped,
tossed away like a cheap toy,
to be played with often
and enjoyed only once:
when ripped to pieces.

Through a keyhole I saw light.
I watched her seek darkness
on a field of rotten rye,
smoking a Marlboro with Salinger.
The door to her was locked.
But each time I loved her
the hinges broke a little more
and a force of nature
stopped her falling from the cliff
deep into razors,
the paint escaping
through tile cracks.

Aeroplanes and Fledglings

Old psalms from young throats
forced me to remember you,
how you sat wide-fingered
on a tryst-worn chesterfield,
heart beating like a fledgling on the pavement.

You were petrified of yourself,
standing like a colonnade
scraping your graffiti
breathing for living's sake—
all of me inside you
to die six months later.

In two hazel mirrors you stood
giving on my mind,
taken by escalator teeth
with the kiss you blew me
leaving your lips
at the speed of mascara
to a sea of exit lights
I drown in
whenever I hear planes.

The Watch and the Hiding

Da bought me a watch
heavy as a guilty throat.
I wore both that day
with a keen wrist and backhand
for I lost it on the dune
doing gambols out of earshot.

I was Ma's angel
but me Da's Divil.
When I said I lost the watch
me Da shouted "Jesus!"
and I screamed, "Jesus!"
followed by Ma.

Jesus came in a buckle:
me Ma came upstairs
pleading for the leather
but Da replied in spittle and steel
and seven lashes
with me sister's age added
for an example.

This went on and on
till forty years later
Jesus took me Da
and I buried him
in me wife's face
beating her
for surfacing me devils.

So what am I?
me wife says nothing,
then I am her silence
and that is that.

Apricots

You touched me last night
like Sikh hands on apricots.
Your eyes, slave-white,
pulled back the voile
for a wounded moon.

I never touched you last night,
my eyes, slave-wet
journeyed through yours,
yet the moon had passed.

We touched again today
like surgeons on my father,
our eyes now imperial
fixed against the voile—
a sunrise blinded us.

Letter from Palermo

I waited for Grandma's high
when she'd call me by her husband's name
until the drugs wore off
and then she'd call me 'Giuseppe',
rubbing herself till I cried.

Syringe-maidens came to keep her comfortable.
She asked for tea to be made in her Ming china cup
and I machined for her a tea
in a plastic cup by plastic sheets.
She whispered 'Giuseppe.'

On her eighty-eighth birthday
Nan crawled by herself to a window,
watched the sun fall like memories,
whispering, I was told, an Italian name
before paling on the golden lino,
clasping a letter sent from Palermo.

I buried her with Grand Papa
but kept her ashes for the South Wind
to take her back to Giuseppe.

The Spider and the Wife

From your lips to mine
you weaved silk in cotton
and a spider crawled
on akimbo shadows.

Every lie was a strand
perfectly formed;
usually on weekends
when guilt forced your lips
on the back of my neck
by the digital flicker—
where the minutes crept
like forgotten heroes.

You screamed my name
yet thought of his,
your web caught me
and I watched you dine on my insides
in a jewel of salt.

I thought of his drooling jaw
curdling the breasts that fed our son.
My wife once sang beautifully
of mockingbirds she'd bring
but then brought a spider and a stepdad
who left when the web was finished.

Cigarette Starlet

  She

  was

my nettle and dock leaf

  my dinner break thoughts

on the swings and slides

    my maths class interruption

      and every sunset shadow
  She

  was

a veil of grey velvet

  the warmth in blood

     calm

       storm

    cigarette starlet

  Now

  we

are miserable

  happy

    heads on a roman statue

      decapitated

        staring

Leaving Crane's Records

David loved Lennon,
expressed it in bass
and his lips were a gauntlet
of beautiful words,
unsung words
that became poems on her lips.

David loved Lynda.
Expressed it in shillings,
buying twelve priceless moments
with twelve unneeded plectrums,
moments that wrinkled
from smiles and old 33s.

Lynda loved to be loved,
expressed this in walking out of Crane's Records forever.
Her heels played bass, tapping out fear
but David changed the song
and in 1969 beneath a Yoko-white veil
three sons and four grandchildren awaited
on lips that lived beyond Lennon.

The Other

I was your bed tortoise
from every dreaded kiss
and only felt your warmth
when inside you
born from Smirnoff on Fridays.

My flesh was like a ferry,
roll-on roll-off.
You would say you loved me,
crowning me a King
of pedestals and guilt.

You were not her,
I was not me.
I was never there:
the other woman was.

When it was all over
your exit was impressive.
The landing light vigil
and mantelpiece memories
facing away from sight,
like the way I slept.

Eight months have passed.
Your hair is short now,
you even wear low skirts.
I feel closer to you at arm's length
for I am not yours,
you were never mine,
the other woman was.
Is.

Harvest Moon

Screams from the shantytown:
locust fog knells in audio horizon.
Wheat bends like chaff bearers
gnawed to origin and silica.
In the hems of the dustbowl
a farmer spills blood beads
from elders' wrists,
chanting at sky.

Shadow walker shimmers,
carries a pail of locusts,
their eyes like garnets on a pyre ring.
These fallen winged scythes
are ground down by peasant teeth,
washed down by prayer.
Tomorrow the elders kill a newborn
with bark from the Acacia:
a handful of seed and with God's grace
a harvest moon.

The January Dogs

Friday:

Savlon death fog rises
and from Kennel 33
a Sheltie-ghost escapes
to mocking grass.

Saturday:

Sam the Labrador pup
holds a child in its eyes.
Waiting by the Volvo
he in turn is held
in the rolling eyes of Shiloh,
his black brother.

Sunday:

Boxer in Kennel 4
French horn barks.
Dash for a name,
question mark by age.
Weight: 5 milligrams
potassium chloride.
Her pendulum tail wags
at a latex executioner.

Room 17, Ashford Hospital

Her cold marbled hand left my grasp
and the changeling appeared
shrieking, "Bastard! Bastard!"

Pristine orderlies arrived.
Her eyes darkened to onyx,
crying for her mummy
as she combed her scalp,
leaving ploughs of coral scurf.

Sedated, she spoke my name,
surrounded by snapshots of bygone holidays
where she'd cover my shoulders from the sun,
looking like a woman
and not a ghost haunted by this life before her.

I leave her with something new,
something from old times,
hoping she'll remember,
knowing she won't.

I kiss her sanguine cheek
whispering I love her,
and she pushes me away smiling
with tears brining her eyes.

Six Million Stars

Two emerald jewels winking
at a man from Leipzig
caressing gold from enamel
like his daughter's hair.

The mountain of heels:
leather canyons,
spilt limb swastikas.
Only clocks march on to Treblinka.

Enter showers mortal,
leave by the chimney,
dressing the sky grey.

Six million stars
wink over Palestine.

Flatline

On bleached shadows
we walked wide-fingered
among polythene faces
and trapped linoleum ghosts.

A skin-pincher marked X
on bar-coded clipboards
where names become numbers
by digital mountains
until monotone.

Limbo makers came
with clichés and syringes
and a fledgling told an eagle
how birds should fly.

I watched the watchers,
mouths like netted fish
murmuring morphine truths
to anyone who'd listen,
and I listened to Bed 16.

Her name was Filomena,
she was 66 years old
and after the driver
she reached back to Galway,
crying "De Valera,"
as the dancing green hills of Wicklow
flatlined.

Blackbird in Bed

Your bleached canvas leaked
to near-death watercolours,
veins broken like splayed cotton
in tapestries of tragedies.

Your face— a blackbird's nest;
your eyes— bird's-egg blue,
a mottled outer shell,
clay smooth to touch
yet tampered yolk
from mouths that kissed you—
they were beaks, tapping to you.

History wrote its Magna Carta
in peppered concaves of insomnia;
eyes clouded like low amp bulbs
distant as willpower
reached out searching mine.

All that arose was draught from peeled sills
yet guilt on your downed arms
was how you viewed yourself—
the blackbird you became.

Your last words, trapped in a clenched fist,
crushing my prayers to a final gasp.
Staring at me, open-eyed,
I saw in your death
how you saw me in life.

Hiroshima, 8:12am

8:12am

From mountain maples
birdsong travelled the delta.
Takaashi made love to his wife
in a scene from a perfect haiku.

8:13am

in the middle of the city
huddled by a wall
an old man sat reading
unaware his shadow would outlive him.

8:14am

A metal stork droned in a blue sky,
Oppenheimer's orphan awoke:
America named it Little Boy.
Sleep, Hiroshima, sleep.

8:15am

Clocks stood still.
Takaashi touched his wife's kimono
one last time, as dust.

Unbroken Horses

My grandfather spat tobacco,
bridling his limbs to stand.
He mixed cortisone and bourbon
raising a beaker to spoiled loaves
saying, "God rest her soul."

I hid his shotguns that day as he looked for bullets,
his quarry, my unbroken horse.
That day I discovered jackals
barked from his bitter tongue:
"You're just like your mother, you fatherless brat."
Truth matures from sour mash.

I hid in the stable with 'Donkey'
but I called him 'Beauty'.
Grandfather never broke him, just Grandma,
when she died face down on fresh linen.

I freed 'Beauty' and wept,
watched him buck and run,
thought of Mum's death
and my murderous birth.

He locked the stable door,
loaded his gun, yelling "Donkey!"
I watched from inside the wooden lattice.
'Beauty' was shot in the hind leg,
tried to stand three times but fell
and Grandfather called me a cissy
only to die on St. Patrick's day
on his knees in vomit, alone
by his broken horse.

Childhood Wedding

I walked upon confetti bones
where hopeless bouquets of roses
touched desperate clambered palms
of the garish unnoticed.

Grandfather wound his watch
coughing blood into ironed silk,
exuding wry misery,
mouth downcurled
like the doomed seams of icing.

Her vanilla gown was lifted,
a ghost of wind racing across a cornfield—
our hesitant kiss on still lips—
Grandfather muttered
to the vol-au-vents.

Blood and Battenberg

Pressing iron to cloth
Nan whistled flutes,
cavalries of blood and mucous.

Pressing lead to tabloid
Grandad scoffed Battenberg,
peeling off the marzipan
quartering the sponge
and only eating the yellow
though he never told me why.

Nan sat down for her programme,
Grandad mashed some tea
balancing a tray of chipped china
and a new pack of cigarettes
that grandma would sniff at,
savouring the deadly veils.

Next summer I found my Grandad
slumped in the elephant chair,
the kettle whistling like Grandma.
Mottled through the steam
he clasped a blood-spotted handkerchief.

The White Disciple

You surface in my languid limbs
like Christ on electrodes
resurrecting me
in nails which caress
and kisses which wound me
each time you leave.

Loss stays
malignant as a tumour.

I will feel you
where your shadow was
whispering in braille rain.

Kefalonia

Those hills behind her
held her innocence
how she held her tongue
when he moaned about her bread.

When she last felt the ocean
it crashed upon her breasts
sixty nine years ago
when she last felt her lover.

One night a year she returns to the hill,
spends a night by the grove the partisans first fell;
waves below crashing like promised bodies
too impatient for tradition.

Tonight the kiln is stoked,
yeast is kneaded like his back
and he will rise in the great loaves.

Bread will be torn,
water will crash
upon her breasts
tonight.

Foxgloves

In the stillness of wheat-packed fields
I walked into skies the colour of barley,
chased the yolky orb
before it hatched silver.
Vixens hung on wire
bowing to their own exposed guts
free at last from the baying hounds,
the genteel savages unleashed.

The sky seemed appropriate,
bloodied and still,
numbed by eerie solitude.
I fell by jellied foxgloves
broken like oaks
at the death of my childhood.

Lost shadows

Shadows merge:
I am totem
statue
painted and black.

I fall
like Saxon castles.
Kindling to two flames,
naked as Godiva.
Nobody looked but her,
numb as a whore's snatch.

We were once a siege of mouths,
burning like Hemingway's lamp
written on the woodchip eyes
of a squandered chance.

Shadows merge, reminding me
that I am darkness,
a lantern of skin,
that only burns
in a pyre of maps.

Monologues

Apostles wrote from your eyes
lamp-black truths
on contorted vellum.

It was there to read:
years of tender abuse
ebonized in anguished doctrines,
the spattered hammer,
the naked bronze cross
lifted till you groaned;
now lazy-eyed,
fallen to pieces
from limp embraces
this Bible with a broken spine
lies beside me
collapsed into folios.

I recite our sins and memories
from pages of dates and times.
Unreachable vows
and selfish monologues
preached by me,
until barren ducts
left rivers on cuffs,
hidden to protect me
until the dam burst
and closed ears finally harked
filleting purity
with Judas glance.

Our love is but a Bible
of broken spines and truths,
a nest of slaughtered dove quills
dripped through skins
leaving a story
no longer believed in.

Sunrise on the Slagheap

Success is a haircut at Toni & Guy
and your flute-tongue for sales
is an orchestra of grief
for the common man you robbed.
Martyrs of the cause
walk black-legged and high-headed
so they can buy a Christmas
before it sells them to the sharks.

Grey-robed skies rinse their wrath:
a blitz of holy water
falls faster than David's sling
on these cowering Goliaths.

Hire a fifty-year-old man for minimum wage,
shake his callused hand
and he will be good to you,
he will sweat blood.
Leave him to machines
and he won't become one
for he is principled
and won't see his grandchildren
grow to be the whip cracker
who broke his back and heart.

Industry,
shine on the slagheap,
on average Joe,
his hocked blood on the black hills.

Corner Shop: Quinton Road

Ravaged by age,
arcing away from skies
pavement slabs roll
until grey becomes green.
Beneath the metal flag
she enters the shelter,
contorting as she sits,
aped by gurning monkeys
who love their grandmas.

Every Tuesday she waits
for the 9:12 to Quinton Road
to hear her name spoken kindly
by David in the corner shop.
Tesco is nearer and cheaper,
full of cantering blurs,
beeps and name-wearing do-gooders
who lower their tone for the palsied,
calling her 'love' if she's lucky.

As she enters the corner shop
the old bell rings,
the heater rattles
and David holds the door
softly speaking her name:
"Hello, Doris."
She crooks her neck to look him in the eyes,
to greet him properly.
Then her eyes damson
at a sign on the wall:
CLOSING DOWN SALE.